THIS BOOK BELONGS TO

_____

New Minimalism Journal

Create Your Plan for a Less Cluttered Life

CARY TELANDER FORTIN
+ KYLE LOUISE QUILICI

SASQUATCH BOOKS
SEATTLE

Tell me, what is it you plan
to do with your one wild and
precious life?

—MARY OLIVER

CONTENTS

YOUR SPACE MATTERS

What you surround yourself with in your home influences how you feel. Changing your surroundings by creating space can shift your entire experience and mood. Or, if you've had a big internal shift and your space doesn't reflect this, sometimes you can feel at odds and out of sync with the very space that is supposed to support and rejuvenate you.

Clearing out old, unwanted, outdated items creates a freedom, lightness, and ease that is better experienced than it is described. It saves time spent searching for objects in your home, dusting them, organizing them, and otherwise tending to them. It saves money, making emotional and habitual purchasing nonexistent. It makes it easier and far more pleasant to host guests, welcome a partner or a child, and engage in the tasks and hobbies that you love.

Each person's ideal space, like their life, is unique; and, we are all best served by having fewer, better things.

———————————

This means we will not be giving prescriptive commands (like thou shall not have more than five pairs of pants!). Instead, we want to empower you to determine the perfect amount for yourself. If you live in Hawaii, maybe two pairs of pants are more than enough. If you live in Anchorage, you might have several times that.

In order to live a life with fewer, better things, you must be able to release the items that no longer serve you. This, of course, is easier said than done. We all know that the objects in our possession are often infused with our emotions and stories. We have attachments to things that run far deeper than the threads of a sweater or the laminated paper of a photo. Which is exactly why we wrote this guided journal.

Throughout these pages we will encourage you to surround yourself with only the things that make you feel the way you *want* to feel. For each person those most sought out feelings will be different. A person who wants to feel serene in their bedroom might remove all artwork from their walls. A person who wants to feel inspired and warm might hang a large, colorful piece of woven fabric on their wall. There is no universal right or wrong; there is only what's best for *you*.

Unpacking your feelings about your home and belongings might feel like an extra step when you want to start decluttering already, but it's this foundational work that allows the decluttering process to be successful. Like an athlete preparing to high jump, it is the coordination of the steps leading up to leaving the ground that make soaring above the bar possible.

The two most important tools for meaningful and lasting decluttering:

self-awareness + self-compassion

(caffeine and large donation bags tie for third).

The structure of this journal reflects the deep work we do as professional declutterers when we're in a client's space. Sure, we spend our days laying out, decluttering, bagging up, and organizing stuff. But what we're really doing is shepherding clients through the process of becoming aware of the thought patterns and habits that got them here. Everything that is currently in your space is something that you said *yes* to at some point. This means that in order to let something go now, you have to acknowledge that either you've changed, your priorities have changed, or maybe it wasn't such a great decision to buy/make/take home that item to begin with.

It's natural to struggle with this process, to feel a little guilt or sadness around having changed or used up resources on something that isn't important to you now. The options now are: (1) to know that this item doesn't serve you any longer, to forgive yourself, let it go, and move forward; or (2) to keep that really expensive shirt with the tags on it in your closet and feel that stab of guilt/wastefulness/shame every time you open your closet door. Your current self is doing the hard work of clearing out so that your future self can benefit from the lightness, ease, and calm that will emerge after all of these leaden items are released.

WHAT'S INSIDE

This journal is organized into two main sections. The first is focused on mind-set. Through a series of guided questions and reflections, you will gain clarity on previously subconscious thoughts and habits. Typically the most challenging part of decluttering is the mental labor of determining priorities and clarifying personal goals. By taking the time to thoroughly answer the questions and process your individual answers, you will have a running head start for the physical work of decluttering.

The second section is where the rubber hits the road: here you will touch every item in your home, decluttering with speed and certainty. Thoughts and emotions will still arise and be a part of this process, but you're going in with a map of your own blind spots and a clear destination in mind: to have in your home only the things that reflect your values and support you in feeling the way you want to feel.

Our wish for you through all of this: an external space that supports, reflects, and honors your highest internal truths.

—CARY AND KYLE
FOUNDERS OF NEW MINIMALISM

PART I

The Mind-Set

The questions on the following pages are meant to illuminate your personal relationship to and narrative about *stuff*. They do this by excavating beliefs, experiences, and habits from your life, as well as the people and cultural forces that helped shape you. Some responses might come to you immediately, while others you might mull over. Whatever your pace, do your best not to judge or censor yourself. While this work is done on the page, its impact will be felt throughout your future decluttered space!

YOUR LIFE
SO FAR

These questions will not be scored at the end; they instead serve to give you a variety of ways to consider and look at your history related to belonging and belongings. Use the space after each question to write down any thoughts, phrases, or memories that come up for you.

How did your home look growing up? Circle all that apply.

SPARTAN

TIDY

PICTURE-PERFECT

EXTRAVAGANT

CLUTTERED

FULL OF INCOMPLETE
PROJECTS

CHAOTIC

OTHER: _____

_____

_____

_____

As a child were you personally:

ALWAYS TIDY   AVERAGE   ALWAYS MESSY

_____

_____

_____

_____

_____

_____

_____

_____

_____

_____

_____

_____

As a child, were you encouraged to try out a number of activities?

☐ Not really. I mostly enjoyed free time to play.
☐ I was only allowed a few activities that I could really focus on.
☐ I always enjoyed trying out new things.
☐ I was constantly busy with different obligations.

_____

_____

_____

_____

_____

_____

_____

_____

_____

_____

_____

_____

_____

How did your home feel growing up?

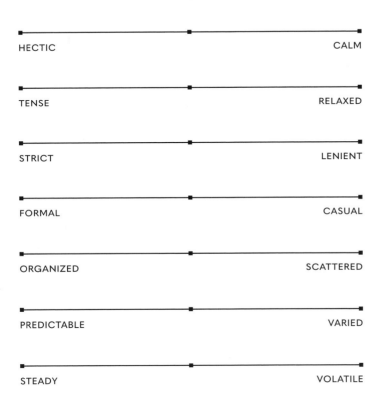

HECTIC — CALM

TENSE — RELAXED

STRICT — LENIENT

FORMAL — CASUAL

ORGANIZED — SCATTERED

PREDICTABLE — VARIED

STEADY — VOLATILE

Did you feel self-conscious about the status or quality
of your home, clothing, or possessions?

ALWAYS, IT WAS   IN PARTICULAR   NOT AT ALL.
VERY PAINFUL.   INSTANCES.

_____

_____

_____

_____

_____

_____

_____

_____

_____

_____

_____

_____

As a family, did you show love through gift giving or
acquiring new things?

NOT AT ALL.   SOMETIMES.   YES, ABSOLUTELY.

_____

_____

_____

_____

_____

_____

_____

_____

_____

_____

_____

_____

_____

Were family finances a concern of yours growing up?

☐ No, I always felt like we had more than enough.
☐ Our finances were in flux at times.
☐ Yes, I was always worried about having enough money.
☐ I don't know—we never discussed finances as a family.

_____

_____

_____

_____

_____

_____

_____

_____

_____

_____

_____

_____

_____

What was your family motto regarding the items in your home?

☐ Waste not, want not.
☐ The more the better.
☐ Gifts should be cherished.
☐ We could use that someday.

_____

_____

_____

_____

_____

_____

_____

_____

_____

_____

_____

_____

_____

Did the community where you grew up value displays
of wealth or associate status with possessions?

■————————————————■————————————————■

NO, NOT AT ALL.   IT DEPENDS—SOMETIMES   OH, ABSOLUTELY.
                   YES, SOMETIMES NO.

_____

_____

_____

_____

_____

_____

_____

_____

_____

_____

_____

_____

How did you feel about your family's economic position in comparison to your community?

| I FELT LIKE OTHERS WERE IMPRESSED BY OUR WEALTH. | WE WERE PRETTY AVERAGE. | I FELT LIKE WE WERE LACKING. |

Did your parents experience any significant economic
fluctuations in their lifetime?

_____

_____

_____

_____

_____

_____

_____

_____

_____

_____

_____

_____

Have you experienced significant economic fluctuations?

_____

_____

_____

_____

_____

_____

_____

_____

_____

_____

_____

_____

Did any of these events impact your outlook on
financial security?

_____

_____

_____

_____

_____

_____

_____

_____

_____

_____

_____

_____

_____

_____

Go back through your answers so far and pull out one to three words, phrases, or feelings that show up repeatedly.

1 _____

2 _____

3 _____

Seeing those words or phrases listed out above, I feel:

☐ Surprised. I don't know that I would have described my childhood in that way before.

☐ Confused. My past experiences seem unrelated or directly in contrast to my current experience.

☐ Happy. I like to think back on my childhood and home life in those positive terms.

☐ A little sad. It's hard to recall some of the more painful or embarrassing portions.

☐ Neutral. I was pretty clear on this story and feel fine about it.

☐ Other: _____

_____

_____

*What else arose for you in answering the questions on the
previous pages? Use the following pages to get all of your
thoughts and feelings out.*

_____

_____

_____

_____

_____

_____

_____

_____

_____

_____

_____

_____

THE ARCHETYPES

When it comes to how we relate to our possessions, each of us tends to fall within one of four distinct personality types, or *archetypes*. We developed these archetypes through working with and learning from our clients. Understanding which archetype(s) you relate to (and thus, where you have trouble letting go) can help shift your mind-set in order to create new habits. Because of their unique characteristics, each archetype has its own admirable strengths and its own set of challenges (what we call the *shadow side*). Depending on their shadow side characteristics, different archetypes can have trouble decluttering certain categories of belongings. Note that it's common to relate to more than one archetype, and different archetypes may feel more relevant to you for different categories. Focusing on embracing the positive sides of your archetype(s) and working to let go of the shadow sides, will give you a framework for working through challenges that might arise during the decluttering process.

Read the questions and circle the corresponding icons to the sentences that you identify with most. You will learn more about the archetypes after this exercise.

1 If you had four hours to work on a project, would you choose to:

- Make a scrapbook of your fondest memories from growing up.

- Create a budget and timeline to help you save up for your dream vacation/clothing item/tech device.

- Write code or engineer a machine to help with a problem you've been mulling over.

- Decide to finish the three fun craft projects you've already started but end up starting a different fourth project instead.

2 Do you save receipts, even for minor purchases, in case something happens to an item?

3 Do you find it hard to say no to commitments of your time and energy, even when you know that you are being stretched too thin?

4 Do more than half of the items in your home remind you of a particular person, a place you traveled to, or an event you attended?

5   Do you hold on to things you don't need because you worry you won't be able to afford to repurchase them in the future?

6   If you look at your most cluttered space, what would you find?

- Bins of cables for unknown electronic devices

- Boxes of items from past hobbies or hobbies you've been meaning to try out

- Receipts and records for important purchases

- Boxes of memorabilia from various times in your life

7   Do others often compliment you on your abundant energy?

8   Are you the go-to person for technical or strategic problems?

9   Does it feel sad, scary, or disrespectful to let go of something that was given to you as a gift, regardless of whether you use or enjoy it?

10 On your walls, you tend to have:

- Shelves for storing tools or other useful objects.

- Framed photos of your family or loved ones.

- Your latest and greatest DIY projects.

- A special piece of artwork you saved up to purchase.

11 Do you conjure elaborate hypothetical future scenarios in which you might need a certain item?

12 You would never get rid of something if:

- You might need it someday.

- Someone gave it to you as a gift.

- It was an expensive item you invested in.

- It's a project you love; you just haven't finished it yet.

13 Is your to-do list long, unwieldy, and some might say unrealistic?

14 Do you feel as though you need to keep every piece of memorabilia associated with a positive experience in order to honor the experience and retain the memory?

15 Do you find it hard to get rid of items that are in some way or another useful?

16 Are you deeply intentional about how you choose to spend your money?

If you circled four or more of the same icons, you exhibit behaviors of that archetype:

CONNECTED

ENERGETIC

PRACTICAL

FRUGAL

Here are the descriptions of each of the four archetypes. Consider how each might show up in your life.

♡ **Connected.** The Connected archetype has an emotional, relational, and impassioned way of approaching the world; they value family, friendships, and partnerships above all else.

- Strengths: relationship focused, sentimental, thoughtful, heartfelt

- Shadow side: clinging

- Challenging categories to declutter: gifts, letters, photographs, and items related to trips, events or celebrations

✂ **Practical.** The Practical archetype operates from the logical hub of the mind; they have a data-driven, methodical, and strategic way of looking at the world.

- Strengths: strategic, deductive, pragmatic, methodical

- Shadow side: limited

- Challenging categories to declutter: art or craft supplies, cords, tools, scrap materials, anything with a perceived use

⚙ Energetic. The Energetic archetype has a physical way of approaching the world; they joyfully move through the world with great stores of energy and zeal.

- Strengths: joyful, enthusiastic, committed, innovative

- Shadow side: Saying *no*

- Challenging categories to declutter: personal and social commitments, projects

🐷 Frugal. The Frugal archetype acts from a place of mindful self-awareness and contentment; they intentionally spend resources on their highest priorities.

- Strengths: self-aware, content, intentional, resourceful, focused

- Shadow side: scarcity

- Challenging categories to declutter: anything of monetary worth, perceived rarity, or invested time

Whether you identify with one or all four archetypes, know that it's not a clutter death sentence; it's actually quite the opposite. Understanding your blocks and tendencies will make it that much easier for you to declutter. Consider this self-knowledge a shortcut to an effective and lasting clear-out.

Below, write out which archetypes you identify with and things you learned that you want to keep track of when you start decluttering.

_____

_____

_____

_____

_____

_____

_____

_____

_____

_____

_____

_____

HOW DO YOU WANT TO LIVE?

When you step across the threshold of your home, what happens inside your body? Do you exhale with relief? Or do you feel tense and overwhelmed? The following questions explore how you currently feel in your home, how you would like to feel in your home, and what changes you need to make in order for your home to support your deepest goals and desires.

Why is now the right time to declutter? How did you decide to take on this project at this particular moment?

- ☐ I'm done being overwhelmed by my space, and I'm ready to make a change.
- ☐ Something exciting is happening in my life, and I want to make more space for it.
- ☐ Something really hard happened in my life, and I'm much clearer on my priorities.
- ☐ I finally have the time to tackle this project.
- ☐ Other: _____

_____

_____

Uncover the feelings you experience when you walk into your home. Check all that apply. When I step across the threshold of my home:

- ☐ I feel disappointed or embarrassed by the status of my home.
- ☐ I wish the space were better utilized.
- ☐ I immediately notice all of the things I need to do.
- ☐ I trip over the pile of shoes/the dog's leash/the unopened mail.
- ☐ I put on blinders and just go to my room.
- ☐ I wish it was different, but I can't pinpoint how it needs to change.
- ☐ I feel like I'm not represented by my home.
- ☐ I exhale with relief.
- ☐ I feel an abiding sense of calm.
- ☐ I feel grateful.
- ☐ Other: _____

_____

_____

Define your why. What are you looking to create in your life? What are you prioritizing by letting go of old stuff, beliefs, and ways of being?

Example:

I'm prioritizing: my physical well-being.

I'm letting go of: my old belief that I should take care of others' needs first and that my well-being is secondary to others' happiness.

I'M PRIORITIZING:

_____

_____

I'M LETTING GO OF:

_____

_____

_____

What are all the feelings that you'd like to experience when you enter your home? Write down all the words that come to mind.

_____

_____

_____

_____

_____

_____

_____

_____

_____

_____

_____

_____

_____

_____

_____

Now it's time to refine this list. Go back to your answers for the last question and circle the three words that are your non-negotiables—these are your Essential Feelings. Write these three words here, along with how you define them. For example, calm could mean that you prefer visual simplicity, it could mean that you want all of your to-dos taken care of, it could mean that you want your body to feel soothed and relaxed, or it could mean something else entirely. There are no wrong words and no incorrect definitions here.

ESSENTIAL FEELING #1: _____

I DEFINE THIS AS:

_____

_____

ESSENTIAL FEELING #2: _____

I DEFINE THIS AS:

_____

_____

ESSENTIAL FEELING #3: _____

I DEFINE THIS AS:

_____

_____

How can your three Essential Feelings be represented in your home? Go room by room, and fill in the same sentence for each space.

Example:

*"To feel the way I want to feel in my **kitchen**, I need: clear counters, to only have tools that are in working function, and to craft a pantry with the basics for only my most-cooked meals."*

TO FEEL THE WAY I WANT TO FEEL IN
MY **KITCHEN** I NEED:

_____

_____

_____

_____

_____

_____

TO FEEL THE WAY I WANT TO FEEL IN
MY **BEDROOM** I NEED:

_____

_____

_____

_____

_____

_____

_____

TO FEEL THE WAY I WANT TO FEEL IN
MY **BATHROOM** I NEED:

_____

_____

_____

_____

_____

_____

_____

TO FEEL THE WAY I WANT TO FEEL IN
MY **ENTRY** I NEED:

_____

_____

_____

_____

_____

_____

_____

TO FEEL THE WAY I WANT TO FEEL IN
MY **LIVING ROOM** I NEED:

_____

_____

_____

_____

_____

_____

_____

TO FEEL THE WAY I WANT TO FEEL IN

MY _____ I NEED:

_____

_____

_____

_____

_____

_____

_____

TO FEEL THE WAY I WANT TO FEEL IN

MY _____ I NEED:

_____

_____

_____

_____

_____

_____

_____

TO FEEL THE WAY I WANT TO FEEL IN

MY _____ I NEED:

_____

_____

_____

_____

_____

_____

_____

TO FEEL THE WAY I WANT TO FEEL IN

MY _____ I NEED:

_____

_____

_____

_____

_____

_____

ARE YOU ASKING TOO MUCH OF YOUR SPACE?

If many categories of belongings exist within one area of your home, it can be a sign that you are asking too much of your space. Note where certain activities tend to take place, and whether or not you need to reassign locations for these activities and their related stuff.

What areas of your home are you asking too much of?

AREA: _____

ACTIVITIES:

_____

_____

_____

AREA: _____

ACTIVITIES:

_____

_____

_____

AREA: _____

ACTIVITIES:

_____

_____

_____

AREA: _____

ACTIVITIES:

_____

_____

_____

Circle the primary activity for each area. Cross out activities you can eliminate from the area.

For example, you may find that the kids always do their homework at the dining table. But when it's time for dinner, they simply shove their homework off to the side. Since they love doing their homework on the large surface, perhaps allow them to continue to use the table, but designate a place where they can put their homework away, like a tall cabinet with areas for each child. Reinforce the habit by having the kids clear their homework in preparation for dinner. Another great example is the guest bedroom that also functions as a home office, off-season clothing storage, and workout space. What is the primary activity that takes place in this room? Is the room set up to support that activity? Only add in additional activities as space allows.

SHARING SPACES   If you share your home with others, take some time to sit down together and have a conversation about how each of you would like to feel in your shared spaces. Some housemates (whether related to you or not) might be slightly resistant to this process. It's helpful to start by offering up what you've discovered about yourself so far, and what's been most surprising and most refreshing. By letting others know what is important to you, you can open up a dialogue for them to consider and discuss what matters to them. The more all members partici- pate, the more likely this process will lead to a cocreated vision for what you *all* want at home.

Conversation ideas:

- If your housemates include an adult partner, room- mates, or adult children, have each person write their own Essential Feelings and lists of how those should be represented in the home (pages 43 to 49). Then, together, create a list of your shared themes, words, or goals. Make sure each person feels represented and that the vision suits all parties.

- If you share your home with older kids (seven and up), sit down to come up with a list of family values for your home. Adults have the final say and will guide the conversation, but enlisting older kids to help define these values or imagine how to create them at home increases their feeling of involvement and ownership in cocreating a decluttered space.

- If you share your home with young children under the age of six, write out your family values on a large piece of paper and then work with your kids to come up with examples of how this might ideally look in your space.

Example: Our values are fun, calm, and nourishment.

Fun means things like building with blocks, dancing, or playing "tickle monster" in our playroom.

Calm means having time to do our favorite relaxing activities, like reading, napping, or playing quiet games, alone or together.

Nourishment means cooking and eating delicious meals together (and sitting at a cleared-off table while we do!).

Our Home

PEOPLE INVOLVED:

_____

_____

_____

_____

_____

OUR SHARED VALUES:

_____

_____

_____

_____

_____

_____

_____

_____

_____

_____

LETTING GO

Before moving on, take a moment to acknowledge all the work you've already done. Now that you're clear on how you want your space and life to feel moving forward, it's time to let go. On this page, write out all of the ways of being, emotions, and beliefs you are ready to let go of. When it feels complete, cut out this page and burn it (safely), shred it, or tear it to pieces.

_____

_____

_____

_____

_____

_____

_____

_____

_____

_____

_____

_____

_____

_____

_____

CUT HERE

By letting others know what is important to you, you can open up a dialogue for them to consider and discuss what matters to them. The more all members participate, the more likely this process will lead to a cocreated vision for what you all want at home.

## PART II

The Process

Now it's time to get down to business! In this section you'll learn the details of the New Minimalism Decluttering Process and use the Project Planning Calendar and Category-by-Category Checklist to keep track of your progress. Consider using a pencil to complete this section to allow for edits. By creating physical space in your home, you clear the path to start living the lifestyle that you really want.

WHERE TO START

You probably have a mental list of things that need to be improved in your home. Here's your chance to get it all down on paper. Take a walk around your home with fresh eyes. Start at the front door and walk through all the rooms in your house. From rooms that aren't working, to drawers or closets you hate opening, to furniture that needs replacing, to lighting (or lack thereof), to behaviors that drive you nuts (why can't anyone hang their jackets on the coat rack?); let it aaallll out. This is your chance to brain-dump everything that bothers you in your home.

TOP FIVE
PAIN-POINTS

Now, organize your thoughts from the venting on the previous page. Look through your notes and circle your top five Pain-Points. List them here; you'll get a chance on the following pages to dig into the specifics of those problems. This will be your prioritized list of where to get started decluttering.

PAIN-POINT #1: _____

PAIN-POINT #2: _____

PAIN-POINT #3: _____

PAIN-POINT #4: _____

PAIN-POINT #5: _____

FROM PAIN-POINTS
TO SOLUTIONS

This is your chance to break down the problems you've listed above and tease apart the individual issues that exist within each.

Example:

Pain-Point that bothers me: The entry

What needs to change: Repaint, create system for bags, relocate mail

Categories that exist here: Jackets, shoes, bags, mail

People who need to be involved: The whole family

Pain-Point that bothers me: _____

What needs to change: _____

_____

Categories that exist here: _____

People who need to be involved: _____

Pain-Point that bothers me: _____

What needs to change: _____

_____

Categories that exist here: _____

People who need to be involved: _____

Pain-Point that bothers me: _____

What needs to change: _____

_____

Categories that exist here: _____

People who need to be involved: _____

Pain-Point that bothers me: _____

What needs to change: _____

_____

Categories that exist here: _____

People who need to be involved: _____

Pain-Point that bothers me: _____

What needs to change: _____

_____

Categories that exist here: _____

People who need to be involved: _____

Go back and circle the categories that appear in more than one Pain-Point. The categories that are mentioned multiple times indicate categories you should start with when decluttering your home. Mark those categories as high priority on the next page, and go from there to create your prioritized list of where to get started.

CATEGORY	PRIORITY TO DECLUTTER:		
	LOW	MEDIUM	HIGH
WARDROBE	☐	☐	☐
ACCESSORIES	☐	☐	☐
KITCHEN	☐	☐	☐
ENTERTAINING	☐	☐	☐
HOUSEHOLD SUPPLIES	☐	☐	☐
TOILETRIES	☐	☐	☐
PAPERWORK	☐	☐	☐
HOME OFFICE	☐	☐	☐
HOBBIES, SPORTS, AND TOYS	☐	☐	☐
SENTIMENTAL ITEMS AND KEEPSAKES	☐	☐	☐
DECOR AND FURNITURE	☐	☐	☐

WHY DECLUTTER CATEGORY BY CATEGORY

We typically declutter a home in the following category order as a way to start with yourself and move outward. If you're having trouble deciding where to start, just use the order below as it's tried and true!

1 Wardrobe and accessories

2 Kitchen and entertaining

3 Household supplies and toiletries

4 Paperwork and home office

5 Hobbies, sports, and toys

6 Sentimental items and keepsakes

7 Decor and furniture

By gathering all items within the same category, you ensure that you fully understand the sheer volume of items you have in a particular category, duplicates are easily revealed, and you don't have to backtrack to a category you thought was complete once you move into a new room. The category-by-category approach allows you to have laser-like focus on a group of specific items in your home, helping you to stay on track and not become distracted by the multitude of categories that may exist within each room of your home.

Start with your highest priority categories from the Pain-Point exercise, but plan to make time to declutter *all* categories in your home, even if you think that certain categories "aren't that bad." Sometimes a client will tell us at the beginning of our work together that they've recently decluttered X category on their own and probably won't purge that much. And yet *every time* we stage and declutter that very same category using the New Minimalism process, the client always replies, "Wow, I didn't think I would get rid of as much as I did!" That's because properly staging each category is extremely effective.

FINISH WHAT YOU START

We recommend blocking off an entire day to begin your decluttering project. Mark the date on your calendar, and hold yourself to it. If you have a whole Saturday, your goal could be to complete your entire wardrobe. Or, if you can't commit an entire day, and you know you only have exactly forty-five minutes on Saturday morning, then tackle all of your shoes, or whatever part of that category you think you can complete in one sitting. Put simply: do not start decluttering if you don't have time to finish it.

HOW LONG WILL EACH CATEGORY TAKE?

Only you can answer this question. There are two variables during the decluttering process:

1   The number of items that exist in each category

2   How long it takes for you to make decisions

To get a sense of your decision-making speed, start with an easy, clear-cut category, like shoes. Set a stopwatch (your phone might have this function) and follow the Decluttering Process on page 74. When you are finished, stop the timer and see how long it took you to complete. This should give you a rough sense of how long each category will take you to declutter.

Recall that the clearer you are on the lifestyle you want, the easier it is to let go of the items that do not serve your purpose, and thus, the faster your decision making will be. Once you are clear that you no longer go on daylong bike rides in favor of more family-friendly physical activities, it is easier to let go of the various objects related to your long-distance cycling days. Not ready to part with them completely? Consider keeping the capsule version of what you need to go on a ride (bike, lock, helmet, basic clothing), but donate all the variations you acquired to bike in the rain, sleet, hot summer days, etc. Keep the momentum, and try not to dwell on your decisions. Let your gut instinct guide you.

DONATION DROP-OFF RESEARCH

Plan ahead and think about the types of items you will probably be donating, and research where those types of donations are accepted by the organizations in your community. Try calling a women's shelter to see if they are in need of unopened toiletries (make sure to ask about those mini hotel shampoos). Local schools often accept age-appropriate art and office supplies (i.e. that extra box of staples, or half of your fancy set of coloring markers). Unopened food is accepted at food banks (ask about specific expiration dates—some organizations accept expired food within a certain timeframe). You will thank your future self at the end of a long decluttering day when you know exactly where to drop off the specific donations, and your community will thank you for your generosity.

Organizations that accept general household
and clothing donations:

Drop-off hours:

_____   _____

_____   _____

_____   _____

Which of the organizations near you accept
these specialty donations:

Drop-off hours:

BABY SUPPLIES _____   _____

KIDS' TOYS _____   _____

ART SUPPLIES/OFFICE SUPPLIES _____   _____

TOILETRIES _____   _____

FOOD _____   _____

FURNITURE _____   _____

SHOWING YOUR LOVE TO MOTHER EARTH: WHAT TO DO ABOUT TRASH?

Unfortunately, not everything you're ready to part with can be sent to your donation center. The items that are expired, broken, dangerous, or too well loved and now deteriorating must be disposed of responsibly. We know it can hurt your heart (and your wallet) to see the now-damaged colored paper you bought for a project go straight into the recycling, or to compost those beautiful spices you brought home from your trip to India. The bright side is that you can transform that pain into lessons learned about yourself and the realities of your time. Next time you're out in the wild about to make a similar purchase, think back to the items you had to throw away during your decluttering session, and change your buying habits accordingly.

For the items that are not donatable, do some research to figure out what materials your waste-management company accepts in which forms. Can you compost expired veggies? What about grains, dairy, and meat? What materials can go into the recycling? Does your provider also conduct bulk pickups? Do they accept something special that you didn't realize, like food donations during the holidays? Write all relevant info on the following pages.

Contact info / website of my waste-management company:

_____

_____

_____

Items accepted—compost: _____

_____

_____

Items accepted—recycling: _____

_____

_____

Items accepted—general trash pickup: _____

_____

_____

Notes (example: your service may provide a once-yearly bulk-junk pickup):

_____

_____

_____

Contact info / website for hazardous-material retrieval:

_____

_____

Note: Never throw hazardous waste (like paint and used batteries) in the trash. This is a separate pickup that might require extra effort.

Items accepted: _____

_____

_____

Special notes (example: closed on Tuesday):

_____

_____

_____

THE DECLUTTERING PROCESS

This process applies to all categories of your house, with three major parts to the process: staging, sorting, and wrapping it up. Each part of the process has detailed instructions. Read through the entire process first so you get the big picture, then reference this as needed when decluttering is underway.

STEP 1: STAGING

This step is extremely important. By first staging your items, you remove them from the context of where they have been living in your home. Seeing everything in one place makes it easier to view with objectivity.

1   Gather all the items in the category from every nook and cranny of your home (yes, that means hunting down your shoes stored in the garage, the attic, the entry, and your bedroom closet).

2   Stage items by placing like with like (all T-shirts are piled together, all pants piled together).

3   Pause and take it all in. Did you realize that you had six pairs of nearly identical black boots? This is your reality check.

4   Clean. Return to the now-empty spaces in your home, and give them a thorough sweep and wipe down.

5   Strategize. With everything now removed from the space, try viewing it with fresh eyes. Use this time to consider your overall organization strategy, systems you need in place, etc. For example, instead of keeping your shoes in six different places all over your house, is there a system that would make more sense and be easier to maintain?

6 Set a goal for yourself. As you appreciate the beauty of your now-empty space, consider what percentage of items needs to be donated so that the space can breathe again. Redefine what it means to be "full" in this area of the house. For a baseline, we typically aim to fill spaces to 50 percent of their *actual* capacity. This guarantees that items stored there are easy to see, access, and put away.

7 Select your favorites. Return to your staged category of belongings. Cherry-pick your top three favorite pieces for the given category, and place them on display. These items epitomize your aesthetic or personal style and will subsequently act as your guiding light.

8 Designate piles. Write the following categories on sticky notes or directly on the bags you will use to sort your belongings:

- Keep

- Donate

- Maybe—this includes clothing items to be tried on. Refrain from pausing the process every time you need to try something on. Save this for the end.

- Recycle

- Trash

- To-do. This includes all the items that:

    – need repair or special cleaning,

    – need to be returned to a store, or

    – you want to sell at a consignment shop.

STEP 2: SORTING   This is where all the decision making comes in.

1   Reference your favorites. Use them to guide your
    decisions. Everything you keep should be able to
    hold its own next to these items.

2   Pick up each individual object, one at a time. (Yes,
    every single item.) As you hold each item, tap
    into your gut reactions—your first impulse. Notice
    what excites you. On the other hand, notice if you
    repeatedly validate *why* something should stay.

3   Decide where each item belongs, and place it in
    the corresponding pile (keep, donate, etc.). Keep
    going until you are finished with the category or
    subcategory.

4   Having a hard time deciding if something should
    stay or go? First remember your Essential Feelings
    on page 44. Let those guide you. Then, reference
    the decision-making tree you'll find on page 81.

The Maybe Pile

The truth about the maybe pile is that if an item made its way there to begin with, it's safe to say you can donate it. The maybe pile is a stepping stone to donating, because there was some lingering doubt that allowed you to put it in the maybe pile to begin with. Look at all the items you are keeping in comparison to that maybe pile. There's a difference, right? Focus on the items that best serve you today, and release past items related to outdated ideas about yourself.

STEP 3: WRAP IT UP   Don't forget to build in time at the end of each decluttering session to wrap up all loose ends. At this time you will undoubtedly be tempted to kick off your shoes, grab a mug of tea (or something stronger), and relax on the couch, but finishing your session with your home clear of items to be dealt with is well worth the effort. Complete the following steps to wrap up your day:

1   Examine your to-do pile. Does it feel exciting or daunting? Be assertive and discerning, because it's entirely counterproductive for you to be left with hours upon hours of projects to deal with at the end of the day! Use your newfound ruthlessness to donate the items that you are wavering over.

2   Return the borrowed items to their original owners.

3   Bring donations to your local donation centers. Make sure to check the hours that each organization accepts donations (these are often different than their normal operating hours).

4   Schedule a time in your calendar for any remaining tasks. Really! Take out your calendar, sit down, and find a day to complete these tasks.

5   Kick back and unwind. We recommend commemorating a job well done by savoring a quiet, easy evening, whether that means taking a relaxing shower, going out for a casual dinner, or cuddling up with a cozy cup of tea or a glass of wine.

DECISION TREE

On the next page is an example of what the decision process will look like when you begin to sort your categories. You'll notice that while some of the criteria is more objective—Does this object function well? Is it in working shape?—many of the questions require emotional clarity. If you're struggling with this part, go back to Part I. Feel free to cut out the page and tape it to the wall while you work for quick reference.

But first . . .

Recall the three Essential Feelings from Part II (page 44). Rewrite them here:

ESSENTIAL FEELING 1: _____

ESSENTIAL FEELING 2: _____

ESSENTIAL FEELING 3: _____

Does this item make me feel the way I want to feel?

NO Donate immediately.

YES Is this item useful/in good shape?

NO Donate or trash depending on item.

YES Do you often wear/use/benefit from this item?

NO Donate pile.

YES Is its value to you equal or greater than the space it takes up?

NO Donate pile.

YES Do you have something similar that has the same or very similar purpose/function that you like as much or more?

YES Select the item you like/use the most and donate the other(s).

NO If you didn't already own this item, would you purchase/make it?

NO Strongly consider donating.

YES Is there an unrelated, higher priority in your life that could benefit from the space (physical or mental) that this item is currently taking up?

YES Donate and repurpose the storage space for your other priority.

DONATE

NO ⟶ **KEEP**

CUT HERE

Redefine what it means to be "full" in this area of the house. For a baseline, we typically aim to fill spaces to 50 percent of their *actual* capacity. This guarantees that items stored there are easy to see, access, and put away.

PROJECT
PLANNING
CALENDAR

Decide on your end-date goal for completing your entire decluttering project. To be realistic, first estimate the number of hours it will take to declutter each category. Then, work backward from your end date, filling in your calendar as necessary to complete each category. Use your regular calendar to keep track of your decluttering project. If you don't use a calendar, this is a great time to start! Google's calendar is useful because it easily syncs to all devices, but a classic handwritten calendar works too!

END GOAL

My house will be entirely decluttered by:

DAY   MONTH   YEAR

_____   _____   _____

My big, fat reward for finishing this decluttering project:

_____

_____

_____

On choosing your reward: Pick something that really excites you! Maybe it's going out to dinner at a fancy restaurant you've had your eye on. Maybe it's a weekend getaway. Maybe it's permission to replace your sagging and tired couch. Maybe it's a self-care day with your favorite way to exercise, a massage, and healthy juices. Make sure to pick a reward that's truly motivating and pick an end date that is realistic without being too easy on yourself. You want enough time while still creating urgency to *get it done.*

As we mentioned earlier, set aside the entire day to declutter whenever possible. We recommend starting first thing in the morning, right after a hearty breakfast and a little caffeine. Don't neglect the setting: Turn on the lights, open the blinds, crack the windows to circulate fresh air, perhaps turn on some background music. And drink water! A couple of hours into sorting, these little tips will profoundly help your productivity and focus.

CATEGORY-BY-CATEGORY CHECKLIST

Next is your decluttering checklist for the typical categories found in most homes. Some blank spaces are included so that you can add your own unique category of say, knitting supplies. Reference the Decluttering Process to make sure you declutter completely and efficiently, and check off the categories as you complete them. Some categories may be easier with an assistant. Having two sets of hands to help you declutter your kitchen or wardrobe can be massively helpful. Try convincing a friend to agree to be your assistant by providing them with a yummy lunch and returning the favor if they need help in their decluttering efforts.

Good luck!

A note on archetypes: You'll see symbols representing the four archetypes next to the decluttering categories listed in this chapter. These symbols are meant to call attention to the archetypes that notoriously have trouble with particular categories. This is a call to be extra mindful and compassionate with yourself when tackling a specific category of decluttering if your archetype appears next to it.

CONNECTED

ENERGETIC

PRACTICAL

FRUGAL

WARDROBE

Most affected
archetypes:

# OF HOURS ESTIMATED	CALENDAR DATE(S) TO EXECUTE	ASSISTANT NEEDED? (Y/N)
_____	_____	_____

The Process

- Stage each subcategory

- Pull top three favorites from each

- Stand strong and proud in your newfound clarity

☐ Tops

☐ Bottoms

☐ Outerwear

☐ Shoes

☐ Accessories

☐ Intimates/Socks

☐ Bags/Luggage

☐ Jewelry

☐ _____

☐ _____

NOTES, ITEMS TO REPLACE,
AND OTHER TO-DOS:

_____

_____

_____

_____

_____

_____

_____

_____

_____

_____

_____

_____

_____

_____

_____

_____

_____

_____

_____

_____

_____

KITCHEN

Most affected
archetypes:

The Process

- Stage each subcategory

- Pull top three favorites from each

- Stand strong and proud in your newfound clarity

☐ Appliances, cookware, and tools

☐ Dishes, glassware, and flatware

☐ Entertaining

☐ Pantry

☐ Refrigerator and freezer

☐ _____

☐ _____

NOTES, ITEMS TO REPLACE,
AND OTHER TO-DOS:

HOUSEHOLD
SUPPLIES

Most affected
archetypes:

# OF HOURS ESTIMATED	CALENDAR DATE(S) TO EXECUTE	ASSISTANT NEEDED? (Y/N)

The Process

- Stage each subcategory

- Pull top three favorites from each

- Stand strong and proud in your newfound clarity

☐ Cleaning supplies

☐ Tools / Utility drawers

☐ Toiletries

☐ Medicine

☐ Linens

☐ _____

☐ _____

NOTES, ITEMS TO REPLACE,
AND OTHER TO-DOS:

HOME OFFICE

Most affected
archetypes:

*Note: This category
can take some time!
Use sticky notes so
that you can stay
organized and easily
categorize paperwork
as you go. Use a
timer and tackle
in forty-five-minute
increments to keep
yourself on task.*

# OF HOURS ESTIMATED	CALENDAR DATE(S) TO EXECUTE	ASSISTANT NEEDED? (Y/N)

The Process

- Stage each subcategory

- Pull top three favorites from each

- Stand strong and proud in your newfound clarity

☐ Office supplies

☐ Media—books, CDs, DVDs

☐ Paperwork—reference materials

☐ Paperwork—magazines and catalogs

☐ Paperwork—financial records

☐ Paperwork—medical records

☐ Paperwork _____

☐ Paperwork _____

☐ Paperwork _____

☐ Paperwork _____

NOTES, ITEMS TO REPLACE,
AND OTHER TO-DOS:

_____

_____

_____

_____

_____

_____

_____

_____

_____

_____

_____

_____

_____

_____

_____

_____

_____

_____

_____

_____

HOBBIES/SPORTS
EQUIPMENT/TOYS

Most affected
archetypes:

FILL IN THE HOBBIES,
SPORTS, AND TOYS
THAT APPLY TO YOU:

# OF HOURS ESTIMATED	CALENDAR DATE(S) TO EXECUTE	ASSISTANT NEEDED? (Y/N)

The Process

- Stage each subcategory

- Pull top three favorites from each

- Stand strong and proud in your newfound clarity

☐ Hobby/Sport/Toy _____

☐ Hobby/Sport/Toy _____

☐ Hobby/Sport/Toy _____

☐ Hobby/Sport/Toy _____

☐ Hobby/Sport/Toy _____

☐ Hobby/Sport/Toy _____

☐ Hobby/Sport/Toy _____

☐ Hobby/Sport/Toy _____

☐ Hobby/Sport/Toy _____

NOTES, ITEMS TO REPLACE,
AND OTHER TO-DOS:

_____

_____

_____

_____

_____

_____

_____

_____

_____

_____

_____

_____

_____

_____

_____

_____

_____

_____

_____

SENTIMENTAL ITEMS/KEEPSAKES

# OF HOURS ESTIMATED	CALENDAR DATE(S) TO EXECUTE	ASSISTANT NEEDED? (Y/N)

Most affected archetypes:

♡

Note: This category can take some time! Use a timer and tackle in forty-five-minute increments to keep yourself on task.

The Process

- Stage each subcategory

- Pull top three favorites from each

- Stand strong and proud in your newfound clarity

☐ Letters and cards

☐ Photos

☐ Keepsakes and trinkets

☐ _____

☐ _____

☐ _____

☐ _____

☐ _____

☐ _____

NOTES, ITEMS TO REPLACE,
AND OTHER TO-DOS:

_____

_____

_____

_____

_____

_____

_____

_____

_____

_____

_____

_____

_____

_____

_____

_____

_____

_____

_____

HOME DECOR

Most affected
archetypes:

# OF HOURS ESTIMATED	CALENDAR DATE(S) TO EXECUTE	ASSISTANT NEEDED? (Y/N)

The Process

- Stage each subcategory

- Pull top three favorites from each

- Stand strong and proud in your newfound clarity

☐ Decorative objects

☐ Art

☐ Plants

☐ Furniture

☐ Collections

☐ Lighting

☐ _____

☐ _____

☐ _____

NOTES, ITEMS TO REPLACE,
AND OTHER TO-DOS:

What If I Fall Behind?

If you don't finish the category within the allotted number of hours you've estimated, then ask yourself: Do you have time to designate another day to this category and still meet your deadline? Do you need to speed up your decision-making process? If you're struggling, refer to the decision tree on page 81, return to your Essential Feelings and desires for your space on page 44, or go for a walk to clear your head. It's OK if the process doesn't go exactly as you planned; what's important here is that you declutter one complete category at a time.

Life happens and sometimes we need to put a project on hold. Be kind to yourself. Forgive yourself if you need to pause this project. Then, when you have space in your life again, come back and move on to the next step in pursuing your goal!

The clearer you are on the lifestyle you want, the easier it is to let go of the items that do not serve your purpose, and thus, the faster your decision making will be.

CREATING NEW SYSTEMS

Every home needs systems to make the wheels go round. The best systems are simple, require few instructions, and can be followed almost intuitively. Any system that requires a lot of instruction, a ton of labels, and a decent amount of time to manage is an immediate red flag. Ask yourself, Is this system requiring too much of my time to maintain? If a complicated system is needed, it is often a sign that a deeper and more thorough decluttering is needed.

SYSTEM BASICS

While each home is unique in terms of its specific system needs, overall there are three basic components to a successful household system. Let's use the example of the entry closet: You want your family to use the entry closet to store their jackets, bags, and shoes, yet there are never any hangers in the entry closet. It is packed full of camping gear, and so the coats, bags, and shoes end up strewn about the house. This system is failing in three specific ways:

1   You are asking too much of the space—in this example, there isn't enough space to use the entry closet to store camping gear in addition to the coats, bags, and shoes. Prioritize the primary purpose of the closet, and relocate the items that are not a part of that purpose.

2   Organizational items are needed—if there are never any hangers in the entry closet, it's unlikely that coats will be hung there. Makes sense, right? Take measurements of the space and snap a few photos on your phone. Armed with this information, procure the *minimum* number of organizational pieces needed (err on the side of fewer). We always recommend searching a local *free* website like BuyNothingProject.org before going to buy these items new. You never know when a neighbor wants to get rid of a collection of perfectly good wooden hangers.

3   A behavior shift is required—maybe you have a system, yet the people involved are not maintaining it. The entry closet is cleared of camping gear; the hangers are there and ready. Yet the jackets remain scattered around the house. At that point it's great to have a roundtable discussion about the topic. Sit down with everyone involved to come up with a system that will work for each person. Come up with a solution that everyone can get behind and modify as necessary.

The best systems are simple, require few instructions, and can be followed almost intuitively.

Here are some common household systems. Feel free to implement any of these tips that speak to you.

SYSTEMS	TIPS
☐ **Incoming mail**	Is your mail opened and sorted right away? Maybe you need a recycling bin near the location you retrieve or process your mail?
☐ **Entryway**	Do you have a landing zone for incoming bags, shoes, coats? Do your keys have a designated home?
☐ **Trash**	Most households have a large trash container and a too-small recycling bin. What if you reverse these?
☐ **Recycling**	It's best practice to rinse and dry your plastic and glass recycling, and separate your paper recycling from the plastic and glass. While your recycling company may not specify this, someone has to do it at some point, and you avoid possibly contaminating the paper recycling with liquids (rendering it unrecyclable) in the process.
☐ **Compost**	Hate the smell? Store food scraps in a paper bag in the freezer. Take it out once the bag is full. This way you avoid the smells and the daily compost run.

SYSTEMS	TIPS
☐ **Household chores**	This is a great conversation for the whole family or all of the roommates. Try assigning chores that work for certain personalities. Rather than rotating chores every week, become a master of your few favorite chores. It's easier to manage when one person is responsible for taking out the trash.
☐ **Laundry**	Laundry no longer piles high when you have the right amount of clothing in the first place. How often you do laundry is going to be a major determinant in the number of clothes you need. If you only wash your clothing every three weeks, then you're going to need a lot of clothing to get you through. There seems to be a sweet spot closer to one week to ten days. We also tend to forget that hand washing is an option in a pinch.
☐ **Dry cleaning**	For your few clothes that might require dry cleaning, try collecting them in a separate part of the closet. Once it's worth a trip to the cleaners, take the whole stash.
☐ **Outgoing items**	For the inevitable items that need to be returned to a friend or brought to a donation center, keep these near the front door, in the way, so that you actually remember to return these items the next time you're heading out.

PLAY DETECTIVE:
IDENTIFY THE
SYSTEMS YOU NEED

Use the evidence of your cluttered surfaces to determine what systems you need. Are your surfaces cluttered with small pieces of paper you don't need anymore? Or small screws and tools from past projects? Do you have a habit of dumping your bag's contents out on a surface and then leaving everything there? Get strict with your habits around these categories of things, and create a home for everything. Use the exercise below to determine if you need additional systems in your household.

Surface/area of the house that's constantly cluttered:

_____

Categories of things cluttering this area:

_____

_____

_____

Surface/area of the house that's constantly cluttered:

_____

Categories of things cluttering this area:

_____

_____

_____

Surface/area of the house that's constantly cluttered:

_____

Categories of things cluttering this area:

_____

_____

_____

Surface/area of the house that's constantly cluttered:

_____

Categories of things cluttering this area:

_____

_____

_____

Surface/area of the house that's constantly cluttered:

_____

Categories of things cluttering this area:

_____

_____

_____

Surface/area of the house that's constantly cluttered:

_____

Categories of things cluttering this area:

_____

_____

_____

From this exercise, which categories make
the most appearances?

THE CATEGORY OF: _____

THE CATEGORY OF: _____

THE CATEGORY OF: _____

THE CATEGORY OF: _____

THE CATEGORY OF: _____

These are the most relevant categories that require
systems in your home.

Brainstorming to
create new systems:

Example:

Category: Wardrobe

System: Removing shoes when we enter the home

System details (include people involved): Get a shoe rack for the entry. Find "inside" slippers that can be worn around the house. At dinner, brainstorm with family ways to get everyone onboard.

1   CATEGORY: _____

SYSTEM: _____

SYSTEM DETAILS (INCLUDE PEOPLE INVOLVED):

_____

_____

_____

_____

_____

2   CATEGORY: _____

SYSTEM: _____

SYSTEM DETAILS (INCLUDE PEOPLE INVOLVED):

_____

_____

_____

_____

_____

3   CATEGORY: _____

SYSTEM: _____

SYSTEM DETAILS (INCLUDE PEOPLE INVOLVED):

_____

_____

_____

_____

_____

4   CATEGORY: _____

    SYSTEM: _____

    SYSTEM DETAILS (INCLUDE PEOPLE INVOLVED):

    _____

    _____

    _____

    _____

    _____

5   CATEGORY: _____

    SYSTEM: _____

    SYSTEM DETAILS (INCLUDE PEOPLE INVOLVED):

    _____

    _____

    _____

    _____

    _____

PAPERWORK SYSTEMS

In this digital era, you probably don't need much paper. Use this to your advantage and unsubscribe from mailings, and move all bill and medical records online. Wherever possible, pay your bills online as well. Many utilities like energy, water, garbage, internet, etc. have online pay options that can greatly reduce your mail. There is a place for the physical paper reminder now and again. But leave those rare papers front and center on a surface as a reminder to pay the parking ticket, renew your driver's license, etc.

Take thirty minutes for each of the following.

TASK:

☐ Unsubscribe from those pesky catalogs . . . they may be gorgeous, but their number one goal is to entice you to buy more. Plus, they are harmful to our beautiful planet. Use Catalog Choice (CatalogChoice.org) to unsubscribe in bulk, or simply call the phone number for the offending companies and let them know you want to be removed from all physical mailings.

☐ Sign up for online bill pay.

☐ Check the *Go Paperless* button on all online accounts (like health records).

☐ Take it one step further, and clean up your inbox. Archive all old emails and when new ones come in, unsubscribe from the ones that you constantly delete and/or never have time to read.

DECLUTTERING YOUR SOCIAL CALENDAR

Decluttering your home is inextricably related to decluttering your social commitments. Often a half-finished
project or abandoned hobby is the sign that you are
spreading yourself too thin across too many commitments and are not finishing one project before starting
a new one.

For the constantly inspired, energetic soul, make a
promise to yourself to not take on anything new until
you finish your already-started projects. Or, when you
decide that you are ready for a new project, say goodbye
to the past one that you never made the time to finish.
If you want *in with the new* (as well as intact sanity), then
you'll need to get strict on *out with the old*.

CALENDAR
ACTIVITY

OBLIGATIONS: FAMILY

_Look at your calendar
for the next four
weeks. Write down all
your commitments;
create your own
unique category
of commitment, if
necessary:_

_____

_____

_____

_____

_____

_____

_____

_____

OBLIGATIONS: WORK

_____

_____

_____

_____

_____

_____

_____

_____

OBLIGATIONS: SOCIAL

_____

_____

_____

_____

_____

_____

_____

_____

OBLIGATIONS: HOBBIES

_____

_____

_____

_____

_____

_____

_____

_____

OBLIGATIONS: VOLUNTEER

_____

_____

_____

_____

_____

_____

_____

_____

OBLIGATIONS: PERSONAL CARE

_____

_____

_____

_____

_____

_____

_____

_____

Write down the activities and hobbies that are not in your calendar, yet you spend time doing anyway (reading, watching TV, social media, meal planning, shopping, cooking, cleaning, gardening, etc.):

_____

_____

_____

_____

_____

_____

_____

_____

_____

_____

_____

_____

_____

_____

_____

_____

_____

_____

Remember those
Essential Feelings
from page 44?
Rewrite them here.

ESSENTIAL FEELING #1: _____

ESSENTIAL FEELING #2: _____

ESSENTIAL FEELING #3: _____

Now, look back at the commitments, projects, and hobbies from your calendar exercise. Circle or highlight the commitments that align with the Essential Feelings you require in your life. Cross out the ones that do not.

While we all have commitments that are not 100 percent fun 100 percent of the time, we *do* have a choice on how we spend our precious free time. Is that time going toward the goals that light up your spirit?

VISION FOR HOW TO SPEND YOUR TIME

Having thoughtfully pared back your obligations and commitments, what will you do with your newly open calendar space and newly clutter-free home? How do you really want to spend your time moving forward? What will take the space of the shopping, returning, and organizing? What will you do instead of those meetings and groups you never really enjoyed?

Imagine your ideal weekday, from morning to night. What are the activities that would fill your day? Get audacious here and really go for it. If you want a weekly massage, write down, "I get my weekly massage!" That's the first step to making it a reality.

MY IDEAL WEEKDAY:

_____

_____

_____

_____

_____

_____

_____

Now, do the same for your ideal weekend day. From start to finish, how are you spending your time?

MY IDEAL WEEKEND DAY:

_____

_____

_____

_____

_____

_____

_____

_____

_____

_____

_____

_____

_____

_____

_____

_____

_____

_____

_____

_____

_____

_____

_____

_____

_____

We know that not every day will be ideal. But now you have a vision of activities and hobbies (reading in bed counts!) that you can integrate into your daily life to make each day align with your Essential Feelings (page 44).

OUT IN THE WORLD

Has anyone ever completed the maze of IKEA without grabbing at least one extra, unplanned item? If you're out there, you must be superhuman.

Marketing teams spend *a lot* of time designing merchandise displays to truly tug at your heartstrings and make you think you need something. Heck, sometimes we don't even know we are being marketed to when our favorite social media influencer recommends a specific product.

The most effective solution? Drastically reducing your exposure to shopping in the first place (unsubscribing from those catalogs and emails is a great start). Don't just think about traditional shopping outlets; also notice what social media platforms or accounts tempt you to buy.

In the following exercises, you will unpack your habits around shopping and the benefits you get from it. And for the times you *do* need to go shopping, be it online or in the physical world, you'll have strategies to outsmart the marketing machines.

EMPLOY A "BUYING MORATORIUM"

To be fair, this isn't just "drastically reducing" your exposure to shopping; it's cutting it out completely. A *buying moratorium* is a defined period of time where you do not buy anything besides food, toilet paper, and any true necessities (medications, deodorant, etc.). We recommend that you enter a buying moratorium for at least thirty days—you can do anything for a month! And, what's the point of bailing water from a sinking ship if you haven't plugged the hole?

This may sound extreme, but drastic times call for drastic measures. If you think about it, since you have had buying power as a consumer, you have been toning and refining your shopping muscle. That's years upon years of shopping. Whether you consider yourself the Yoda of consumption or you feel slightly out of control with your shopping habits, quitting shopping cold turkey for a set amount of time is an incredible way to gain deep perspective on when and where you are tempted to buy.

I WILL ONLY BUY FOOD AND ESSENTIAL LIFE ITEMS
(LIKE TOILET PAPER AND MEDICINE) FOR _____

                                    # OF DAYS

BUYING MORATORIUM BEGINS: _____

                          DATE

BUYING MORATORIUM ENDS: _____

                         DATE

IN-PERSON TIPS FOR GOING COLD TURKEY:

- Avoid hanging out at shopping destinations, like the mall.

- If you have to buy, shop from a predetermined list and don't veer from it.

- See something you love? Take a photo of it and then Put. It. Down. Often times you forget about the item after a day or two.

ONLINE TIPS FOR GOING COLD TURKEY:

- Unsubscribe from emails you receive regarding online sales.

- Block websites that are your favorites to buy from.

- Unfollow materialistic-minded influencers (you know, the ones who always endorse new products).

- Create a Pin board on Pinterest to tag things you love and want to remember later. It's the same tactic as the photo idea. You'll find that your impulse to buy fades with time (it's like magic!).

Remember, you can love and appreciate something without owning it.

Include any items that really tempted you to buy. Do these particular items relate to your Essential Feelings? No self-judgement here, just observations about what came up for you during this process.

FEELINGS, EMOTIONS, AND DESIRES I NOTICED
DURING THE BUYING MORATORIUM:

_____

_____

_____

_____

_____

_____

_____

_____

_____

_____

_____

_____

SHOPPING HABIT TRACKER

Now that your buying moratorium is complete, it's time to dig into the specifics of how you like to shop. Some stores or particular scenarios are our personal kryptonite. These are the places where we cave and typically walk away with more than we intended. What stores are your personal kryptonite? Don't forget the grocery store and online shops. Those count too! By understanding the emotional reward you get from shopping and teasing it apart from the actual act, you will be able to move from reactive, habitual *shopping* to intentional, thoughtful *acquiring*.

List all stores or scenarios that are your personal kryptonite and the emotional reward you get from buying in those scenarios. What were some stores or scenarios that made you feel tempted to shop during your buying moratorium?

KRYPTONITE SCENARIO: _____

_____

REWARD: _____

KRYPTONITE SCENARIO: _____

_____

REWARD: _____

KRYPTONITE SCENARIO: _____

_____

REWARD: _____

KRYPTONITE SCENARIO: _____

_____

REWARD: _____

The point of this line of reflection is to highlight how shopping has turned into an inconsequential pastime for many of us. Often we shop because it feels good. But that hit of dopamine you get each time you swipe your credit card fades quickly, leaving you to constantly chase that good feeling with more and more shopping. We find it is best to let go of shopping by replacing it with a different, gratifying activity (one that is aligned with the Essential Feelings you listed on page 44). It can be hard to break a habit, so it is helpful to have your default replacement activities lined up and at the ready.

Examples: Go for a walk to my favorite park, bake cookies with (insert loved one here), plan my next vacation, read a novel, or volunteer at a charity I hold close to my heart.

ACTIVITIES I CAN DO, OR PEOPLE I CAN CALL, INSTEAD OF GOING SHOPPING:

1 _____

2 _____

3 _____

4 _____

5 _____

**ARM YOURSELF
WITH EMOTIONAL
STRATEGIES**

If you do have to go out into the world and expose your-self to all that tempting merchandise, develop a shop-ping mantra.

Examples:

- Are you easily enticed by sales?

  "I already have everything that I need."

- Do you love to treasure hunt or browse online?

  "I can appreciate beauty without needing to own it."

- Are you accustomed to continually bringing in new items to your space?

  "Fewer, better things."

- Do you find yourself stocking up on useful goods?

  "The store can hold my future belongings; I only buy what I need right now."

MY SHOPPING MANTRA:

_____

_____

_____

GIFT-GIVING PHILOSOPHY

The act of giving someone a gift feels good; there's no doubt about that. But now that your newly decluttered lifestyle is more focused on experiences and relationships rather than things, it only makes sense to extend that philosophy to the gifts you give to others. So how will you embody your version of minimalism, while still honoring your friends and family? The intention behind any gift-giving—the thought, care, and attention paid to the giftee—can (and should) be honored; the gift itself is not important.

MY GIFT-GIVING PHILOSOPHY:

_____

_____

_____

SOME IDEAS:

- I will only give gifts that can be eaten.

- I will only give a gift that I know my giftee is in need of and will use all the time.

- I will give the gift of my time for a shared experience.

- I will give gifts with the caveat, "If you find you don't use this, please feel free to pass it on."

- I will donate to worthy causes in people's names.

135

SOUVENIR PHILOSOPHY

Traveling and memorable experiences often entice us to memorialize the event with a physical object. But to retain an object for every trip you ever take for your entire life is just asking for a space that is cluttered with stuff. Steer away from the tourist-trap collections (think the mug or snow globe with the city's name). Instead, treat purchases on your travels as you would any other purchase—with extremely high standards, focus, and intentionality. Maybe you've been looking to replace your oversized comfy sweater? Keep an eye out for one on your next trip.

MY SOUVENIR PHILOSOPHY:

_____

_____

_____

SOME IDEAS:

- I will first and foremost savor the trip or experience as it is happening.

- I don't need a physical object (or photo) to make my memories real and lasting.

- Tchotchke-like collections have no power over me; I can admire their cute factor and refrain from owning it at the same time.

SAVOR THE MOMENT

A regular mindfulness practice goes hand in hand with minimalism. Mindfulness, or some form of meditation, brings space and attention to the thoughts that may have otherwise been reactive or spiraling. These are the same reactive thought patterns that have been addressed throughout this journal. Start with simple breathing exercises to bring you out of your head and back into the world around you, and experiment till you find a form of meditation that resonates with you. It's the practice of savoring the moment and living fully with people and experiences that create a meaningful life.

SOME MINDFULNESS PRACTICES:

- While sitting in a comfortable position, inhale for the count of seven, pause at the top of the breath, exhale for the count of eight. Continue for ten breaths.

- Write down one thing you are grateful for every morning.

- Make it a regular practice to open the windows, pause, inhale deep breaths of fresh air, and take a moment to look around and see what's happening out there.

- In the evening, throw on some layers and go outside to watch the setting sun.

CONGRATULATIONS!

Yes, you did it! You've successfully completed the *New Minimalism Journal*. We hope that you've uncovered things about yourself that you didn't know before, that you've discovered some blind spots and now better understand how you relate to your things. It's a good sign if this journal looks like it's gone through the wringer—written all over, with words crossed out, circled, and highlighted—the physical evidence revealing the personal epiphanies you've had along the way. We hope you continue to use the tools and strategies from this journal to create space in your home and in your life.

Know that there will be peaks and valleys along your path toward minimalism. As you continue to explore and prioritize what values and activities you hold dear, regularly check in with your home and habits to make sure your current lifestyle is reflected in your surroundings. Your personal version of minimalism will grow and evolve as you do.

The amazing thing about minimalism is that it's a tool always at your disposal. As you enter new phases of life, evolving and shifting as a person, you can return to this process to reinvigorate your space. Any time you find yourself overwhelmed by the pace of life, the demands of your day, or the amount of stuff in your home, know that this journal is here to guide you back through the process of restoring calm and ease to your life.

NOTES

ACKNOWLEDGMENTS

For Lark + Brady

To Hannah Elnan: Our match was pure kismet. Your editorial skills and dedication are surpassed only by your patient, kind intelligence. To the entire team at Sasquatch and Penguin Random House for their vision and execution, for helping to imagine this book and share it with the world, with our whole hearts: thank you.

To our New Minimalism community—our clients, readers, and friends: Whether new to the family or original NM devotees, we are grateful for you. Your dedication to this work and creating a beautiful, healthy, kind world inspires us to keep fighting this mindful fight.

To our families, both born and chosen: It's your unconditional love and unequivocal support that steadies and buoys us through the hard times and the good. You being you is why we can be us.

To Cam and partners; our guinea pigs; our patient, loving, and handsome other halves: what an honor to walk through this life with you by our sides.

ABOUT THE AUTHORS

CARY TELANDER FORTIN specializes in the psychology behind decision making and attachments, as well as environmental and social advocacy. She graduated with honors from Dartmouth College with a degree in psychology.

KYLE LOUISE QUILICI specializes in creating beautiful spaces using the items clients already own and love. She graduated from Boston College with a degree in human development, studied interior design at Parsons School of Design in New York, and earned her certificate in sustainable design from UC Berkeley Extension.

Together as **NEW MINIMALISM**, Cary and Kyle have conducted hundreds of decluttering sessions and as a result they have donated tens of thousands of cubic feet of clothing, art supplies, furniture, and decor to local charities.

Looking for more guidance on creating your own definition of minimalism and simplicity? Check out Cary and Kyle's book *New Minimalism: Decluttering and Design for Sustainable, Intentional Living*, which includes even more information about all aspects of the journey, from archetypes to case studies to design principles!

Printed in China

SASQUATCH BOOKS with colophon is a registered
trademark of Penguin Random House LLC

23 22 21 20   9 8 7 6 5 4 3 2 1

Editor: Hannah Elnan
Production editor: Bridget Sweet
Design: Anna Goldstein

ISBN: 978-1-63217-265-5

Sasquatch Books
1904 Third Avenue, Suite 710
Seattle, WA 98101

SasquatchBooks.com

MIX
Paper from
responsible sources
FSC® C008047